What people are say

"This book is for you if you are not a Christian but you're seeking answers, or if you are a Christian who is struggling with the tough questions of life. Intelligent, honest and compassionate, reading this is like having a conversation with friends."

Rebecca Manley Pippert, author of *Out of the Saltshaker*
and *Uncover*; founder of Saltshaker Ministries

"An excellent book that answers some of the hardest questions about the Christian faith, and keeps coming back to Christ to do so. Read it, then give it to your friends so they can read it."

Rico Tice, Associate Minister at All Soul's Langham Place,
London; founder of Christianity Explored Ministries

"Straightforward, down to earth and Bible-based, a good introduction for anyone in their twenties or teenage years who is looking for answers on some tricky issues."

Jon Fenton, Senior Research Fellow, London Centre for
Nanotechnology at University College London

"This book brilliantly articulates the concerns we have, and distils complex answers into easily digestible chapters."

Nick McDonald, blogger at Scribblepreach.com and Youth Pastor at
Carlisle Congregational Church, Massachusetts

"I love this book! It tackles the big questions and shows how ultimately only Jesus makes sense of things."

Jonty Allcock, Pastor of Bush Hill Park Community Church,
London; author of *Lost* and *Fearless*

"A really easy read that answers challenging questions in a loving but honest way. I would definitely recommend this to you if you have questions about Jesus, and what it means to follow him."

Lottie Jones, Youth Pastor at St George's Leeds, England

"Michael and Carl do not run from tough questions—they face them with humour and above all a clear conviction that life makes sense when Jesus is allowed to speak for himself."

Glen Scrivener, evangelist and blogger

Tricky

**The hardest questions
to ask about Christianity...**

...and some answers

**Michael Dormandy
and Carl Laferton**

thegoodbook

COMPANY

Michael Dormandy lives in Oxford with his wife, where he's studying for full-time ministry at Wycliffe Hall. He enjoys reading, drinking coffee and eating cake. He used to work as a teacher.

Carl Laferton is Senior Editor at The Good Book Company and lives in London with his wife Lizzie and two young children. He used to be a sports journalist and a teacher, and loves all sports except darts.

Tricky
© Michael Dormandy / The Good Book Company 2014.

The Good Book Company
Tel: 0333 123 0880; International: +44 (0) 208 942 0880
Email: info@thegoodbook.co.uk

Websites
UK: www.thegoodbook.co.uk
N America: www.thegoodbook.com
Australia: www.thegoodbook.com.au
New Zealand: www.thegoodbook.co.nz

ISBN: 9781909559172

Design by André Parker
Printed in the UK

Contents

Welcome to *Tricky*

In the olden days (20 years ago), people sent messages with a pen and paper. When they wanted to know the news or sports results, they bought a newspaper. When they took photos, they had to take them to a shop and wait for them to be developed before they could discover that they were all out of focus. And people used plastic rectangles a bit bigger than this book, called videos, to watch films.

Now we can do all these things in seconds, using something half the size of this book. As Bob Dylan sang: "The times they are a-changin". (If you don't know, Dylan was a singer from the days before iPhones or even videos).

Many people think the Christian faith belongs with videos. Old, outdated, irrelevant. It's a leftover from a time that's gone. It doesn't really have a place in our world of iPads and google and social media.

And yet... not *everyone* thinks like that. In fact, a lot of people think the opposite. We've met people from all nations, all ages, all religious backgrounds and all personality types who have found themselves drawn to the man at the centre of Christianity, Jesus.

And that's really strange. Here's a guy who lived 2,000 years ago, worked as a carpenter, never left his home state, and died as a criminal. Yet here we are, in a very different world, and what he said and what he did is still the subject of dozens of films, and books, and arguments. Some love him. Some hate him. But, unlike all the other carpenters who lived in the middle east in AD1, almost everyone has some opinion of him.

So it makes sense to ask questions about Jesus—about who he really was (and whether we can really know), what he really said, and whether and how it matters to you. Maybe you know Jesus made some extravagant promises about life and eternity—but you really don't think you can trust that they're true. Maybe you've only just started looking into it, and you want to see if the whole Christianity thing stands up to reason. Maybe you're pretty sure it's all rubbish, but you're willing to give him the time it takes you to read this book before you make your mind up. Maybe you've been brought up being told Christianity is true, but you have your own tricky questions and they're not going away.

That's why we wrote this book, and why we're thrilled you've opened it up. It's great to ask questions. We ask them ourselves. If Jesus is who he said he was, he won't be embarrassed by questions or afraid of them. He might not always give the answers we'd like, but he'll give the best answers we can get.

So in this book, you'll find the hardest questions that we think anyone can ask about Christianity. And in each chapter, we'll see what Jesus has to say in answer to them. Of course, a book this length doesn't tell you everything there is to say. But we're aiming to help you think things through, get your head round Jesus' answers, and see what you make of them.

You can read the chapters in any order—just start with the one that most grabs your attention, and go from there.

Two more things. First, whenever you read "I" in a chapter, "I" means Michael, because he supplied the stories. And second, we want to say a quick, but very big, thank you to everyone who's helped us with the book. We wish we had space to name you. But we don't, because people reading this book want to get on with thinking about the tricky questions.

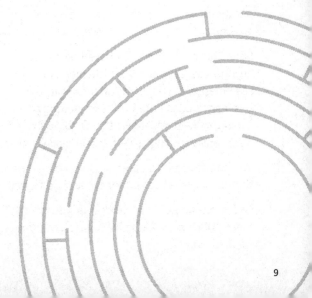

1. Doesn't Jesus spoil your fun?

Let us introduce you to ourselves and to some of our friends. Lots of us have bad hair. We wear clothes that haven't been fashionable for decades (if they ever were). We like country dancing and we love board games. We occasionally play poker, but never, ever for money. Some of us quite like sport, but we're too nice to be competitive. What we'd call radical, you'd call dull.

We're not really like that. But that's the image we think lots of people have of anyone who takes living Jesus' way seriously. Because isn't being a Christian about becoming a bit more boring than you otherwise would have been? Doesn't following Jesus spoil your fun?

Christians can come across as boring, restricted or just a bit strange. Church has got itself a reputation for being where the dull people hang out. But here's the thing: when Jesus, the founder of Christianity, lived on earth, he didn't get accused of being boring.

In fact, the opposite happened. People told Jesus off for having too much fun.

Here's what people said about him:

> "Here is a glutton and a drunkard, a friend of tax
> collectors and sinners."   (Luke chapter 7 verse 34*)

"A glutton"—someone who loves good food so much that he's never far from the "all you can eat" restaurant. "A drunkard"—someone who's always at the bar. "A friend of tax collectors and sinners"—the people in town who don't bother with the rules, live how they like, enjoy spending their money, and ignore the authorities. That's what people said about Jesus: *You eat too well, you drink too much, you hang around with the crowd that has too much of the wrong kind of fun.*

The serious types around in Jesus' day really didn't like him. Why? He enjoyed himself too much. He wasn't boring enough!

Have life

In the Gospel of John, one of the four historical biographies of Jesus' life, his first miracle was to produce a large amount of something. What do you think he made? Hymn books? No. Board games? No. Charity publicity? No. He made wine. Really good wine, out of really boring water. About 800 bottles of really good wine, to be enjoyed at a wedding reception.

Jesus was accused of a lot of things. But never of being boring.

And Jesus wanted to share the joy around. He didn't make the wine for himself, but for others. He didn't come to enjoy his own life, but to give others that kind of life. Here's what he said he was all about:

> "I have come that they may have life, and have it to the
> full."   (John 10 v 10)

---

* To help people find their way around the 66 books that are in the Bible, someone helpfully once split it into chapters, and then split the chapters into verses. So Bible references are followed by the name of the book, the chapter number, and then the verse number.

Jesus is offering life. Not merely lungs-working, heart-beating, brain-working kind of life (we've got that already), but life "to the full". Life at its best. Life that lasts for ever. Life as it should be lived.

Aren't we all looking for this kind of life? I'm guessing you want a life that's full, instead of empty—exciting, instead of boring? Well, this is exactly what Jesus promises. We don't have to tell Jesus to get a life; Jesus gives us life.

Our culture tends to have an image of Jesus as quite a dull man, coming to take the life out of life. Don't fall for the fake. The real Jesus came to put the life into your life.

But what does this look like in practice? Well, to give "life to the full" Jesus does three things.

1. Jesus says "yes" to good things.

Jesus wants people—you—to enjoy life. God filled the world with good and fun and beautiful things. He made some wonderful stuff to see, smell, taste and do. Then he gave that world to you and me. And he said: "Enjoy!" He told us to enjoy the world, enjoy each other and enjoy life. What things do you do for fun? Chances are at least one of those things is mentioned positively in the Bible. The Bible tells us to enjoy drinking and dancing, food and friendship, exercise and art.

Yes, but... what about sex? One part of life where Christians have a really anti-fun reputation is sex. Maybe you've heard that Christians think sex is disgusting, embarrassing, even scary. Doesn't the Bible tell us not to talk about it, not to enjoy it, and not to do it unless absolutely necessary?

Erm... not really. Here's Exhibit A: the first command God gave to the first man and woman:

"Be fruitful and increase in number."   (Genesis 1 v 28)

In other words, have sex and have kids!

Here are Exhibits B and C, taken from two books in the Bible written to show how to enjoy life and relationships to the full:

> "May you rejoice in the wife of your youth.
> [She is like] A loving doe, a graceful deer—
>   may her breasts satisfy you always,
>   may you ever be intoxicated with her love."
>
> (Proverbs 5 v 18-19)

> "My beloved is … outstanding among ten thousand …
> His body is like polished ivory …
> His mouth is sweetness itself;
> he is altogether lovely."   (Song of Songs 5 v 10, 14, 16)

According to the Bible, sex within marriage is an exciting, beautiful and precious gift. God encourages us to enjoy it. He even encourages husbands to delight in their wife's breasts and wives to love looking at their husband's body—if that makes us giggle, it just shows we're far more embarrassed about sex than God is! Like with a lot of good things in life, you might think Christians hate sex. You might be right about some Christians. But Jesus says yes to good things. After all, that's why he made them.

2. Jesus says "no" to bad things

Perhaps you've been thinking: "OK, you say Jesus says yes to good things. But then why are there still so many things Christians aren't allowed to do?" Then you reached the first three words of this subtitle—"Jesus says no"—and thought: "Aha! Here comes the catch. I knew it—being a Christian is about Jesus telling me not to do things."

And you're right—there are things Jesus calls us not to do. There are things Jesus says no to. He tells us not to get drunk; not to have sex with people we aren't married to; not to gossip about other people. And he also tells us not to be those really annoying people who don't get drunk or sleep around or gossip, but spend the whole time looking down on people who do.

No one likes to hear the word "no". And Jesus does say "no" to things. It looks what we might call "burdensome"—a bunch of commands weighing you down, stopping your fun, squeezing the joy from life.

But let's be honest—sometimes a "no" is for our good. Every parent says no to their young children sometimes. When I was a child, I received hundreds of "no's", which were for my good:

"No, you can't play near the oven when it's on."

"No, you can't run across the road without looking."

"No, you can't put the cleaning chemicals near your mouth."

In other words, there are commands that aren't a burden, but are a blessing. I'm grateful for my parents' "no's"—if they hadn't bothered to say them, I'd probably be a burned, squashed, poisoned wreck by now.

The Bible claims that Jesus' commands are in this category: "His commands are not burdensome" (1 John 5 v 3). And when we think about it, we can often begin to see why Jesus' "no's" are for our good.

Getting drunk gives you a headache, wipes your memory, empties your wallet, and prompts you to do things you'll regret the next day. Long term, it wrecks your body. Jesus says there's a better way to enjoy a night out, to have fun, and to feel confident, which doesn't rely on alcohol—so he says a loving "no" to getting drunk.

Sex outside marriage leads to broken hearts, broken trust, and sometimes even broken bodies. Jesus knows that it's better left for marriage, where it can be relaxed, secure, free… and more fun. So he says a loving "no" to sex outside marriage.

Talking about people behind their back might feel great at the time, but it leaves you unable to trust others, and leaves others unable to trust you. So Jesus says a loving "no" to gossiping.

But what about when we really can't see the reason for Jesus' "no"? What about when, however hard we think about them, his commands just seem unfair and unkind? I can get drunk every now and then without causing any problems, so why does the Bible say no? It's such hard work to talk to the lonely people, so can't I just sit with my friends? These commands feel so burdensome.

In the end, sometimes we have to trust Jesus that his commands are for our good, even when it's hard to understand. When I was about six, my mum was in hospital with a severe and very infectious illness. I wasn't allowed to go near her, because of the risk of infection. I had to look at her through a glass window. As we drove to see her, my dad explained all this to me—but I was six, I knew how life worked, and I wasn't buying it. She was my mum! She couldn't do me any harm. For me, that was enough. And so my father sat there in the car, arguing with a stubborn little boy who refused to accept his dad might know more about life than him. His commandment, his "no", was for my good, even though I couldn't understand why.

Sometimes Jesus says no to things we really want. That's when we ask ourselves: "Do I trust him? Do I trust that his "no" is for my good?" And that's a good question to ask. The way to work out the answer is to get to know about him some more—to see if Jesus is the kind of guy whose commands you can trust. Why not get to know him better? You can start by reading one of the accounts of his life in the Bible.

It's great that Jesus says yes to good things, and shows us how to enjoy them fully. It's good that Jesus says no to things he knows are bad, even if we can't see why. And yet there's something even more amazing that Jesus does…

3. Jesus says "Yes" to the best thing
We all want to have fun. We make decisions based on what will make our lives most enjoyable, now and in the future.

But sometimes the fun fades. The parties get dull, the friends move away, the sporting victories feel hollow. Sometimes, the fun runs out. We face illness, bereavement, relationship breakdown, failure in an exam or in a job.

Maybe the fun's run out for you at the moment. Some of us experience hopeless loneliness and bullying. Some of us feel we're never good enough (particularly if others are telling us we're not). Some of us feel we've made so many mistakes, we'll never sort life out. Some of us live in terror that we won't be able to find a relationship, a job, or a house, or money. Let's face it; even if we pretend to other people that we're fine, none of our lives are full of fun, all the time.

And all of our lives will end one day. Death isn't fun. But it is, sadly, where we're all headed. All the experiences and enjoyment of our lives now will come to a full stop. Death kind of gets in the way of fun.

Following Jesus is, as I've said, not nerdy or boring—it's enjoyable, and it's fun. But there's far more to knowing Jesus than that. Remember why Jesus came:

> "that they may have life, and have it to the full."
>
> (John 10 v 10)

Jesus offers more than fun. He offers life, and life to the full. When we feel lonely, he'll be with us. When we feel we're not good enough, he'll tell us we don't need to be; he loves us. When we feel guilty about past mistakes, he'll promise we're forgiven. When we're worried, he'll tell us he provides for us. Finally, when death wraps up the fun of this life, Jesus can give life for ever with him, when all the hard things will be gone and there is only joy.

When you look at it like that, you begin to see that Jesus doesn't ruin our fun. Quite the opposite: he gives us life.

2. In the end it's just a matter of opinion, isn't it?

I love coffee. I just love the smooth, rich, warm, bitter taste in my mouth. I also like peanut butter. It's so creamy, nutty and full of flavour.

On the other hand, I hate photocopiers. I can somehow never get them to work without the machine spewing out hundreds of pages with the back photocopied on top of the front. I don't like rice pudding either. It's just too gooey and gloopy for me.

Total truth and arguable opinion

You and I can disagree about coffee or peanut butter. You might rather jump into a nest of killer ants than drink a cup of coffee. No one can say that you're right and I'm wrong—because these things are just individual opinions.

But some things are a bit different. We can't disagree about whether Mount Everest is the tallest mountain in the world or whether Germany won the 2014 World Cup or that John Adams was US President in 1800 (I had to look that one up). If we disagree about things like that, one of us will be wrong. This is because these things are true; they're not just an opinion.

Many people today think that beliefs about God are just opinions. Some of my friends in London went to a school where there were different school assemblies for the different religions in the school. They each sang their own songs, had a short talk about their own belief system, and prayed their own prayers. Christians went to the Christian assembly, Jewish students to the Jewish assembly, Buddhists to the Buddhist assembly… you get the idea. This school treated ideas about God as opinions. Friday afternoon was sports, and you picked a sport: football, basketball, hockey. It was your choice, your opinion. And then Monday morning it was assembly time, so you picked what you wanted: Christian, Jewish, Muslim, whichever you liked. It was your choice, your opinion.

The truth test

An important way to tell the difference between truth and opinion is that truth is *testable*. If something's true, you can test it and prove that it's true. You can work out the heights of all the mountains in the world and prove that Everest is the highest. It's scientifically testable. You can see the TV footage of the World Cup Final or even talk to people who were there, and find out what happened. You can look into all the evidence that John Adams really was President in 1800. These things are historically testable.

On the other hand, even if you and I sat and drank a hundred cups of coffee and ate a hundred jars of peanut butter, I couldn't prove they were nice, and you couldn't prove they were horrible.

Many people think God can't pass the truth test. After all, we can't see him or touch him, so it seems there's no way to prove that God exists, or that the Bible is true, or that Jesus offers eternal life. If they can't be tested, they can only ever be opinions. Unless…

Unless God's visited us...

Unless God had come to earth. Unless he had met people, and spoken to people, and been written about by those people. Then we could test him, just as we can test other historical events and people.

And that's exactly what Christians claim happened. Here is the beginning of a letter written by a friend of Jesus called John:

"That which was from the beginning, which we have heard, which we have seen with our eyes, which we have looked at and our hands have touched—this we proclaim concerning the Word of life." (1 John 1 v 1)

The only person who's been around from the beginning is the person who created everything else—God. So when John says he's heard, seen and touched someone who was around at the very beginning, he means he's heard, seen and touched God himself. And his name is "the Word of life"—which is one of John's favourite names for his friend Jesus.

John is saying that in Jesus, God's Son became a human who lived, walked and talked. People could meet him and test him and find out what he's like.

This means that what Christians believe might be true or untrue, but the one thing it can't be is just an opinion. I can't prove to you that coffee is nice, because I can't see, touch or test niceness. But I can prove that Germany won the 2014 World Cup Final, because people were there who saw the teams line up, saw the game go into extra time, and finally saw Mario Götze score the winner for the Germans. You can choose not to believe them. But then you'd just be wrong!

And in just the same way, there are people who say they saw Jesus walk and talk and teach and do things only God can do. They are either right, or they're wrong.

Does Jesus really pass the truth test?

What Christians believe is either true or false, rather than an opinion. So the big question is: *Is it true or false?* The way to decide that is to look at the evidence. We all believe Germany won the World Cup—even though we weren't there and may not have even seen the game. Why? Because many reliable journalists were there, and they reported it. That's the evidence for the World Cup result.

So, what's the evidence for Jesus? Well, it's found in the documents that are contained in what we call the Bible.

a. Eye-witness evidence

The first stage of the truth test is to ask: "Did the authors of the documents actually see Jesus, or were they just making up stories?"

There are four books in the Bible recounting the life of Jesus, which are traditionally called "Gospels". They are named after the people who either wrote them or gave lots of the information behind them. Here are the words from the beginning of the third, Luke's Gospel. He helpfully tells us how he put it together:

> "Many have undertaken to draw up an account of the things that have been fulfilled among us, just as they were handed down to us by those who from the first were eye witnesses and servants of the word … since I myself have carefully investigated everything from the beginning, I too decided to write an orderly account for you, most excellent Theophilus, so that you may know the certainty of the things you have been taught."
>
> (Luke 1 v 1-4)

When Luke was alive, there were many reports about Jesus and many came from eye witnesses. And he had thoroughly looked into all the evidence and was writing a careful account of what had happened, based on what he'd learned from people who actually saw it.

The fourth Gospel is by John, who wrote the letter we looked at earlier in this chapter. Towards the end of the book, John writes:

> "This is the disciple who testifies to these things and
> who wrote them down."   (John 21 v 24)

John says: *I can testify—witness—to these things, because I saw them. Now I'm writing them down.*

But how do we know that Luke and John, and the writers of Matthew's and Mark's Gospels, really were telling the truth? After all, if they were Jesus' friends, wouldn't they be tempted to exaggerate or even lie to boost his reputation? If that's your question, it's a really good one! But here's the thing: these guys, and all of Jesus' closest friends, were prepared to suffer and die rather than stop claiming that their friend Jesus was God. If it was all fake, and if they knew it was a fake because they'd faked it themselves, surely they would have admitted that rather than being killed.

If the Gospels were guesswork, then the Bible, and what it says about God, would be just a matter of opinion. But they're not— they're written by people who saw Jesus and touched Jesus. He passes the first part of the truth test.

b. Careful copying

But even if the reports about Jesus were accurate at the time, how do we know the versions we have today have stayed accurate? Could they have been changed along the way? After all, it was 2,000 years ago!

For books from the ancient Roman period, like the Gospels, we don't have the original bit of paper that the author himself first wrote on. But this first piece of paper was carefully copied lots of times and then those copies were carefully copied lots of times, and then those copies… and so on. What we have today are loads of these copies, called "manuscripts".

Did mistakes ever creep into the copying? Yes, and sometimes the manuscripts disagree with each other. How can we know which are right? Scholars think about the age of a manuscript, and where it was copied, and how many of the other manuscripts agree with it. I did a little bit of this myself one summer, when I worked on a letter by a church leader from the 1600s called Bartholomaeus Holzhauser (they had good names back then!). I spent hours peering at scanned photographs of different versions of the book and then comparing them, on one occasion trying to work out if Holzhauser had written "had built" or "have built". Textual scholarship needs experts (and I was a mere beginner!), but in the hands of an expert it can be done accurately and well.

But it can only be done well if there are large numbers of copies (so there's as much evidence as possible), and if those copies were made near the time of writing (so that inaccuracies have minimal time to creep in). And this is where the Gospels win in a World Ancient Manuscripts Championship.

There are 24,000 manuscripts containing some or all of the New Testament. That thrashes any other book of the period (the runner-up is the ancient Greek poem, *The Iliad*, with just 650). And the earliest Gospel manuscripts come from within a few decades of the original, as compared to centuries for the other writings.

Does this mean the scholars are always absolutely sure that every verse of our New Testament always definitely says what the original writers wrote?

No. Thoughtful Christians should admit this. But none of the doubtful verses are secret and none of them are significant. Many people like to say that the church has lied about the Bible and that secret, more accurate versions, which portray Jesus very differently, exist in a locked vault somewhere. This kind of story makes for good movies, but not for good reality. All the different possible readings are listed in what are called "critical editions" of the New Testament, which you can buy in academic bookshops. Many are also listed in the footnotes at the bottom of the page in a Bible. They are also all irrelevant to the important things Christians believe.

For example, in Matthew, chapter 6, verse 33, Jesus says: "Seek first his kingdom". Some manuscripts say "Seek first the kingdom" and others say "Seek first the kingdom of God". Scholars aren't 100% sure which is right, but it doesn't actually matter that much! In the context, Jesus obviously meant the kingdom of God, not anyone else's kingdom, so we needn't lose sleep over whether he said the actual words "of God" or not.

If the Bible versions we had today had been changed through the centuries, our ideas about Jesus would all just be matters of opinion. But what we read is what they wrote; and so Jesus passes the second stage of the truth test.

c. Trustworthy translation

If the New Testament is so accurate and we can know what it says, how come there are so many different versions around today? You can get loads of different English translations, dozens of different Spanish ones, many Mandarin versions, and so on. And that's because the Bible wasn't originally written in English, so there are lots of different ways it's been translated. Since the translations differ, surely we can't know that any one of them is right, can we?

But let's take a single French phrase:

J'aime jouer au football.

Someone could translate it in loads of different ways:

I like to play soccer.

I like to play football.

I like playing football.

I love to play football.

They all mean the same thing! They all communicate the same truth. And good translations of the Bible (the ones I tend to read are called the *New International Version* and the *English Standard Version*) are like that—they are communicating the same truth, and say the same thing. They're not different opinions—they're the same truth about Jesus. Jesus passes the final stage of the truth test.

Unbroken chain

There is an unbroken chain linking us trying to work out what's true in the 21st century to the days when Jesus walked on earth.

Jesus, who is God himself, walks on earth

People who saw him and touched him write down his life-story

This story is accurately copied for 2,000 years

Scholars iron out any inaccuracies that have crept in

The Bible is well-translated

Our Bibles today tell us accurately about a time when God walked on earth and you could see him and touch him

We can have opinions about God if we want to. We can come up with our ideas and preferences. But that's not what the Bible is doing—the New Testament is offering us evidence—testable claims and historical evidence that the God who made the world came and lived in it. And the evidence about him is written down and is in your hands when you open a Bible. Which makes the Bible amazingly exciting!

But...

This chapter has concentrated on the New Testament. But of course that's only about a quarter of the whole Bible—the Old Testament is much longer, and it's often much more difficult to accept that it's not just a bunch of opinions of ancient writers. Even if the New Testament is reliable, rather than opinion, how can we possibly think the Old Testament is, too?

This is where Jesus is really helpful. When Jesus had a discussion or a debate, he often quoted the Old Testament. Once, when he was asked a question about marriage, he replied:

> "Haven't you read ... that at the beginning the Creator
> 'made them male and female,' and said, 'For this
> reason a man will leave his father and mother and be
> united to his wife...'?"   (Matthew 19 v 4-5)

What's important here is that Jesus tells the people listening to him to read the Old Testament. And then he says that in the Old Testament, "the Creator ... said"—even though that bit of the Old Testament isn't a speech by God, it's a comment by the human writer. So Jesus is saying that when we read the Old Testament, we're not just reading a human's words—we're reading God's words, that he inspired a human to write down.

If Jesus is right, the Old Testament is true in all it says about God and about how we're to live. And if Jesus is right, it's also true in all the facts it teaches. So, when it seems to contradict science or archaeology, we have to work hard at thinking through what it's really saying, and how that fits with what we see in the world—if God made the world and God wrote the Bible, then they won't contradict each other.

Sometimes this means seeing that something in the Bible is using imagery, it's not aiming to be taken literally—like, for example, where it says: "The eyes of the Lord [God] range throughout the earth" (2 Chronicles 16 v 9). Other times, we might realise that a scientist or a scholar is biased against the Bible, so that what they say is skewed. Other times, it might mean accepting that we just don't know the answers, but that we do know what Jesus said about the Old Testament being God's word. And if we decide that the New Testament is trustworthy, and that Jesus is God, then we can trust what he says about the Old Testament, even when we find it hard to understand.

An even bigger but...

But the really, really big problem is that the Bible says the strangest things about Jesus himself. It says he fed 5,000 people with five loaves of bread and two fish. It says he healed the diseased and the disabled with just a word or a touch. Most amazingly of all, it says he rose from the dead. Can we really believe things like that, however good the evidence is?

That's what the next chapter is about...

3. How can anyone believe Jesus rose from the dead?

I am 11 and it is my first day at a new school. I am nervous and excited, sitting in my first assembly. And the headteacher suddenly starts talking about an older boy called Ben who has died of a heart attack over the summer holidays. I've never met him; I've never even heard of him before, but he is dead. I am starting at a new school and someone else has just left it. He's dead.

I don't know Ben, so I'm not quite sure how to feel, but I know I feel shocked. This was supposed to be an exciting, optimistic day, and now there's a faint black cloud in the background. Death does that.

Seventeen years later, I am 28. I have been married for just a couple of months, and we've just moved to Austria. Life is exciting. My wife has left for work and I am about to boil my eggs for breakfast. I am looking forward to a normal day, when suddenly I get a message to phone my Mum. I ring straight away. She is in tears and can hardly talk. She tells me that she thinks my Dad has died. A few hours later it's confirmed—one of the wisest, bravest, most loving people I have ever known has gone. I will never see him or talk to him again in this life. Dad is dead.

Once again, I'm shocked; and once again, I really don't know how to feel. Once again, an exciting and optimistic time of new possibilities is damaged, but now the black cloud isn't on the horizon—now, it fills everything I can see. Death does that.

You're probably thinking this is a depressing way to begin a chapter. And you're right! But it's also realistic. We don't talk about death much. We don't like to think about it, either. And yet everyone experiences it. Death is one of the most shocking, painful and hard-to-deal-with realities we face. But face it we must.

The only question is, how?

A happy ending

Christians believe that Jesus has beaten death. He died like everyone else, but then he came back. And that completely changes the way a Christian looks at death. Imagine a nasty school bully who has you cornered. Now imagine you have an older, bigger brother; he walks into the playground and smacks the bully so hard that he screams and runs. No one will fear the bully in quite the same way again. He's still nasty, but there is hope. The Bible says this is what has happened with death. The strongest and kindest elder brother ever, Jesus, has defeated the worst bully in the history of the world.

So Christians have a new attitude to death. It's still nasty, it still hurts… but there is hope. It can be beaten, because Jesus has gone through death. He died, and then three days later he came back to life. There is a happy ending to life, not just a black hole and a coffin.

OK, OK, but… really? Fairy stories all have happy endings. The problem is that they're not true. And it's perfectly understandable for you to read what I just wrote—"He died, and then three days later he came back to life"—and think: "How can anyone believe that? I don't believe Cinderella really had a glass slipper, lovely though the story is. I don't believe there's a world in which Shrek exists, fun though that would be. And I don't believe there's a historical day on which a man called Jesus started off dead and finished off alive."

So, why do Christians not believe in Cinderella or Shrek, but do believe in Jesus coming alive again?

Because of the evidence. That's the difference—evidence. Let's look at how we can know that Jesus rose.

Tomb empty

Jesus was executed on a Friday. On the Sunday morning, his tomb was empty. This is in all four of the eyewitness accounts in the Bible, the "Gospels". There are slight differences between them, but this is just what you'd expect if a number of different honest witnesses gave accounts of a real event.

And when, just over a month later, Jesus' friends stood up just a few miles from his tomb and said that he had risen from the dead, no one went to get the body. There were a lot of people who didn't like the idea of Jesus rising. If the tomb hadn't been empty, they could simply have given some guided tours of the tomb and shut Jesus' friends up.

But they didn't. The tomb was empty.

So what happened to the body? People have come up with lots of theories over the years.

Perhaps someone moved it? Grave robbers, perhaps—and yet, when the empty tomb was found, people "saw the strips of linen lying there, as well as the cloth that had been wrapped round Jesus' head. The cloth was still lying in its place, separate from the linen" (John 20 v 6-7). The linen and cloth were expensive—that's what a robber would have stolen. What kind of burglar breaks into a tomb, takes what is heavy and worthless (the body) and leaves what is light and valuable?!

Did Jesus' enemies move it? Again, surely if they'd moved the body, they would have admitted it and put it on display, because they were desperate to stop people following Jesus.

So, maybe Jesus' friends took the body and faked the rising from the dead to help them start a new religious or political movement. They must have dreamed of being rich, powerful and popular… but they suffered hatred, violence and death because they claimed he had risen. Accounts from the time suggest that all but one was killed violently because they claimed Jesus had risen. If they'd faked it, why not just admit it and spare themselves all the suffering?

So if no one took the corpse out of the tomb, maybe there never was a corpse? Some people have claimed that Jesus didn't actually die when he was executed. They say he was only nearly dead, and recovered in the cool of the tomb and escaped. But Jesus had been whipped until he was virtually dead. Then he had nails the length of coffee cups driven through his wrists and feet. Then he was hung on a wooden cross for hours. After all that, his executioners thrust a spear into his side. Do you think he would be able to roll away a massive rock, beat an armed guard and walk off?

The strange facts are that there was a corpse in a tomb. Then there was an empty tomb. But no one had moved the body.

And then the appearances started…

Man appears

Many people saw Jesus after he had risen from the dead. Once he appeared to over 500 people at the same time.

The people who saw Jesus alive again weren't stupid. They knew dead people do not come back to life. When Jesus appeared for the first time to some of his closest friends…

> "They were startled and frightened, thinking they saw a ghost."

But he wasn't a ghost…

> "He said to them, 'Why are you troubled, and why do doubts rise in your minds? Look at my hands and my

feet! It is I myself! Touch me and see; a ghost does not have flesh and bones, as you see I have.' … They gave him a piece of broiled fish, and he took it and ate it in their presence." (Luke 24 v 37-39, 42-43)

Jesus appeared to many different kinds of people on different occasions. Could these appearances have been hallucinations, weird dreams or people's minds playing tricks? No—the encounters were too widespread and varied for that.

The only explanation is that Jesus rose from the dead, just as he had predicted months before:

"The Son of Man [Jesus' way of talking about himself] must … be killed and on the third day be raised to life." (Luke 9 v 22)

And, on that Sunday morning in history, he was.

But dead men *DO NOT* rise!

Many times in my life, I've been angry and frustrated with God. I've wanted to stop being a Christian. I've experienced doubts. But I've only rarely doubted the facts.

One time I did was in my third year at university. I was studying Philosophy as part of my course, and I left a session with one of the lecturers with serious questions about whether or not Jesus rose from the dead.

The problem the lecturer posed me, and that I struggled with, was this: no amount of evidence should ever make you believe in something that's impossible. If something's impossible, then even if the evidence for it is strong, it can't be true. Pigs don't fly. So if you see a pig in the sky, then even if it looks just like a pig, you must be mistaken. It must be a balloon painted to look like a pig, or a very oddly shaped cloud in red sunlight. Pigs just can't fly, so it certainly isn't a pig.

In the same way, even if there's really strong evidence that Jesus rose, it can't have happened because dead people just can't rise.

It's a powerful argument. It really shook me. But after a while, I realised that the argument assumes that a man rising from the dead is impossible. It starts off by believing that it's impossible, and then it concludes that it obviously didn't happen. But this is the opposite of being open-minded. It's like deciding one day that it's impossible for a dog to bark. If you decide to believe that, then every time you hear a dog bark, you won't believe it. It must have been a car back-firing. It must have been an mp3 recording of a bark. It must have been a human doing an impression of a bark. You would conclude that it is just coincidence that whenever you hear a bark, there's always a dog nearby with its mouth open. This is what happens when you assume that something is impossible.

Obviously, there's a big difference between assuming dogs can't bark and assuming dead people can't rise! Lots of biology suggests the dead can't rise, while no biology suggests dogs can't bark.

But if God does exist, then he controls biology. That means he can overrule biology. If there is a God, he can raise the dead. And you would expect it to be a very, very rare thing, rather than an everyday kind of thing. In fact, it would be a great way for God to show us that a particular man is particularly special—that he is, in fact, God himself.

If there's even a possibility that God exists, there's a possibility that a man could rise from the dead. So it's open-minded to listen to the evidence; and the evidence is strong. It may seem unlikely; but if every other explanation is more unlikely, or simply impossible, then you're left with… Jesus rising.

So if you're not at all convinced about Jesus rising from the dead, it's worth looking at the events of what we now call Easter Sunday, and asking yourself:

"What do I have to believe in order to *not* believe Jesus rose from the dead?"

And then ask yourself if what you do believe is more unlikely, more far-fetched, than God raising a man from the dead.

About six years after that lecturer made me doubt, I heard he was ill with cancer. I wrote him a letter saying I'd enjoyed his teaching and trying gently to tell him more about Jesus. I got no reply, but later learned that he died. I really hope he changed his mind. Otherwise, death defeated that man because he ignored the man who defeated death.

A real happy ending

I hope I've made it clear that there are lots of good reasons to believe that Jesus rose from the dead. But... so what?

There are many reasons why Jesus rising from the dead is important. Open the New Testament, the second part of the Bible, at a random page and you'll probably find a few. Here are just some:

Jesus rising shows that he is who he claimed to be: God come to earth.

Jesus rising shows that what he says, and promises, is true.

Jesus rising shows that we should think very carefully about being on the wrong side of him.

And, wonderfully, Jesus rising means that we don't need to be worried about death. Shortly after my father died, I sent an e-mail out to some friends, containing these words spoken by the risen Jesus:

> "Do not be afraid. I am the First and the Last. I am the
> Living One; I was dead, and now look, I am alive for
> ever and ever! And I hold the keys of death."
>
> (Revelation 1 v 17-18)

Jesus is saying he has defeated death and holds its keys. It's as if death is a dungeon in which we are all prisoners, and Jesus has the key. In fact, Jesus is the key. He said:

> "I am the resurrection and the life. The one who believes
> in me will live, even though they die."   (John 11 v 25)

In other words, anyone who trusts in Jesus will live for ever, beyond their physical death.

That's why, though I miss him, I have confidence I will see my father again. That's why, though death is painful, I don't fear it, and you don't need to either. Life can have a happy ending, and it's no fairytale. It's based on historical, wonderful, true fact.

4. If Jesus is real, why is there so much suffering?

> "[Rukshana's] husband threw acid on her. Then her sister-in-law poured petrol over her. Finally her mother-in-law took a match and set her on fire. A cerise and gold veil hangs over her head, its delicate glamour in stark contrast to her ruined face. She still lives with her attackers, she explains, because otherwise she could not afford to care for her sick children."
>
> (I read this in *The Economist* in March 2012)

Those words come from an article about domestic violence. They make us scream at the evil in the world. They make us think: "Why doesn't someone do something? Why does this have to happen again and again?" In other words, Rukshana's story makes us ask one of the most difficult questions in this book:

How can there be a God of love in a world of suffering?

For many of us, it's not even the suffering around the world that makes us wonder how God can be there. It's the suffering in our own lives, our own families, and our own friendship groups. The loneliness of broken homes. The confusion and shock of bereavement. The tragedy of serious illness. The cruel humiliation of being bullied. Don't these all make us cry: "Where is God? If Jesus was real, he'd do something right now"?

Compared to many people, quite possibly compared to you, I haven't suffered that much. I've known the pain of broken relationships, the very real threat of career failure, and family bereavement. These didn't exactly make me question whether or not God was there, but they did bring me to times of emotional darkness, when I had no idea what God was doing or why.

In this chapter and the next, we will explore some of the things the Bible says about pain and suffering. I'm taking two chapters over it, because it's such an important and difficult question. What does the Bible say about suffering?

The *past*: an explanation for suffering

The Bible tells the story of how suffering came into the world. It comes in Genesis chapter 3—within the first few pages of the whole Bible. When God first made the world, his verdict on it was that it was "very good" (Genesis 1 v 31); there were no problems and no pain. God created the first two people, Adam and Eve, and gave them a beautiful garden to enjoy. (It can seem a bit difficult to fit this story with science, so if that's a question you have, flip to chapter 6). Adam and Eve could do whatever they wanted, except eat from one particular tree, because that tree symbolised deciding what was right and wrong. If they ate from that tree, they would be saying that they, not God, could make the rules and run the world. God had created a world that was very good and had given it all to them to enjoy. The only thing they had to remember was that it was God's world, and he was in charge.

Here's what happened next:

> "When the woman saw that the fruit of the tree [the
> one that symbolised deciding what was right and

> wrong] was good for food and pleasing to the eye, and
> also desirable for gaining wisdom, she took some and
> ate it. She also gave some to her husband, who was
> with her, and he ate it."   (Genesis 3 v 6)

They disobeyed. Both Adam and Eve decided they, not God, would run the place. And in doing so, they wrecked the place, not just for their lifetimes but for the whole of the rest of human history.

How does Adam and Eve doing one bad thing long ago ruin the world for everyone else, ever since? The Bible says that their disobedience—the Bible's word for it is "sin"—had a number of consequences. First, humanity was ruined; and second, the world was ruined. People are ruined because when Adam disobeyed God, disobedience entered our bloodstream. We all started doing it, instinctively, like a ball falling on the ground when you drop it. It never takes me any effort to be lazy, selfish or big-headed. It just comes naturally. The Bible says it started with Adam, and that it continues in us. We are sometimes the victims of other people disobeying God and hurting us. We are often the people who do the disobeying and hurt others or ourselves. The Bible's quite blunt about this:

> "All have sinned and fall short of the glory of God."
>   (Romans 3 v 23)

So the sad fact is that we're all like Adam.

Think of the world as a theatre musical. A brilliant writer-director-composer has written a masterpiece script. The costumes, props and lighting are realistic and stunning. All the actors make you feel that the story is completely real. In the upbeat moments, the music is so catchy you hear it in your head for weeks afterwards. When it looks as if the guy's going to leave her, the girl sings a song that makes your eyes go moist. It's the greatest musical ever written.

But then, on the first night it's being performed, the main actor gets drunk. The director has warned him not to, but he does it anyway. He mistakes his lines and blunders into the props and set, breaking them; he can hardly sing in tune; the plot of the play is mangled completely. The masterpiece is trashed by one man's disobedience—and everyone suffers.

The same is true of our world. We live in a messed up masterpiece, messed up by one man disobeying God, and continually messed up by us disobeying God.

This story raises lots of questions: and the Bible doesn't answer all of them. That's because the Bible's not actually *most* interested in why there's suffering in the world or where it came from—it wants us to focus on what God's going to do about it and how he helps us in the middle of it. In other words, the Bible doesn't always give us answers; instead it gives us hope and help. And when you are suffering, you will probably want answers, but you'll want hope and help a whole lot more.

The *future*: freedom from suffering

The Bible promises that one day God will reverse the consequences of humanity's disobedience. He will restore the masterpiece he's made and end all suffering. The end of the Bible describes an amazing future scene:

> "[God] will wipe every tear from their eyes. There will be
> no more death or mourning or crying or pain, for the
> old order of things has passed away."
>
> (Revelation 21 v 4)

Everything that could possibly be wrong in this world, from the minor to the serious, will be gone, but everything good will still be there. Fire will barbecue burgers, but never trap babies in buildings. The sea will be there for us to sail, swim and surf, but never to drown people. Work and study of all kinds will challenge and excite us, but never be boring, frustrating or too difficult. People will be united in love and never divided. Our bodies will be perfect and healthy and we won't look in the mirror and feel only despair.

But best of all, Jesus will be there. The one who loves us more than we could ever imagine—the one who has remade this world for us to live in—will be at the centre of the creation, and we will know and experience his love completely.

Why hasn't this happened yet? As I said earlier, we don't always know the answers to questions like this, because the Bible's more interested in hope and help than complete answers. But part of the answer is that God is waiting so that as many people can be there as possible. God is giving people time to trust in Jesus, so they can enjoy life in this perfect world too, instead of being shut out of it.

After all, don't you want to be part of this perfect world? Doesn't suffering make you hunger for it? The pain and hurt of life aren't a reason to reject Jesus; they're a reason to trust him and be part of the wonderful world he will make.

The *present*: the message of suffering

Think back to the Bible's account of how suffering entered into our world—through Adam disobeying God. All suffering is the result of one human being, Adam, doing something wrong. This tells us that suffering in general is humanity's fault, because Adam was a human, but it also tells us that your individual suffering isn't necessarily your fault.

Of course, sometimes people bring their own suffering on themselves through their own wrongdoing. If a murderer suffers life imprisonment, his wrongdoing has caused his suffering. In this sense, it's deserved. But that isn't the kind of suffering that makes it hard to believe in God—the kind of suffering that seems undeserved.

Let's go back to the story of the drunk actor. Imagine, as he staggers through a dance routine, that he lurches off the stage and into the orchestra pit. His left-foot narrowly misses a violin, but his right foot tears right through a bass drum, wrecking an expensive instrument. Is the drummer more to blame than the violinist? Of course not. The drummer wasn't more guilty than the violinist, just more unfortunate.

This has an important consequence: apart from situations like the imprisoned murderer, suffering has a general message for everyone, but a particular message for no one. Jesus made this point when he was talking about some people who died when a tower collapsed on them. He said:

> "Do you think they were more guilty than all the others living in Jerusalem? I tell you, no! But unless you repent, you too will all perish." (Luke 13 v 4-5)

Jesus is saying that people who suffer aren't necessarily suffering because they're worse than anyone else. Suffering usually isn't a message from God to the individual person suffering, telling them they're particularly bad.

I'm afraid to say that Christians often get this badly wrong. Maybe you've heard Christians say that AIDS is God's punishment on gay people and sex workers; or that the devastation caused in 2005 by Hurricane Katrina was God's punishment on gamblers in New Orleans. This is a cruel and insensitive way to respond to suffering and if it's hurt you, I'm so sorry. It's exactly what Jesus doesn't say. If you're suffering at the moment, I don't know why it's happened to you, and not to me. I do know it's *not* because God thinks I'm better than you.

But Jesus is saying that suffering does have a message to the world in general. What is that message?

> "Unless you repent, you too will all perish."

"Repent" means turning to Jesus and beginning to follow him. Suffering reminds us that the world is messed up. The solution God has given to the ruined world is Jesus' new world. When we see suffering in the world or feel it in our own lives, we long for it to be over. We long for a world where that pain doesn't exist. And Jesus says we can enjoy that world, if we repent—if we turn to him, the loving ruler of that world, who when he lived and died and rose again did everything necessary to open the way for us to be part of that world. (By the way, if you're not sure what you think about Jesus rising from the dead, head to Chapter Three).

So, when we read about a woman like Rukshana, in the story at the start of this chapter, this should stir our hearts with compassion, frustration and even anger. It should remind us of how horribly messed-up our world is. It should make us turn to Jesus, who will one day repair our messed-up world.

And that should make us want to help people like Rukshana, because that's what Jesus tells us to do. He is committed to removing suffering, and he commands his friends to have the same commitment. Christians haven't always been good at obeying Jesus on this one, and I'm sorry if Christians have let you down when you've needed help. But Christians have also done some amazing things. Recently, I had the opportunity to visit a centre for ex-drug-addicts and alcoholics run by Christians. There are people who've been abused from a young age and have descended into despair, which has led them to drink and drugs. At Betel, they have a loving family environment, daily meetings to get to know God, hard manual work, strict rules, and a chance to experience the loving power of God. Many break free from heroin, and stay free.

The people who started Betel are Christians. They have seen suffering in the world. They have responded by turning to Jesus. They have shared his commitment to helping others, both by making things better in their present and by pointing them to Jesus' perfect future world.

Any better ideas?!

There is no easy answer to the question of suffering. You may not like the Bible's answer. But let me ask you to think about what the alternatives are.

Everyone deep down has an opinion about suffering. But if we reject the reality of God, then we're rejecting future hope and we're losing any reason to help now. If all human beings are is a random, pointless collection of blood and organs, thrown together by accident, then there's no reason to care when other people suffer, and no reason to hope when we suffer ourselves. There's no real reason to try to ease others' pain, except that we'd like to be treated that way if we were suffering (which is, if you think about it, quite selfish).

I don't think that we naturally want to answer the question like that. Jesus has a much better answer to offer. His answer begins with "repent" and it ends in a perfect new world.

5. Does Jesus care about my pain?

Two friends of mine, a lovely, caring couple, lost their first child to sudden infant death syndrome (SIDS). He was eight months old.

Another friend lost both his sisters in their twenties.

Another experienced problems as a teenager that were not of his own making, but which wrecked his education. He has been living with the consequences for decades.

When we look at situations like this, our hearts break. We want to do something, or even just say something, that will make things better, but we don't know anything we can do or say. The tragedy just seems to overwhelm anything positive.

We care, but we can't do anything. But if God is there, then he could do something. So maybe he doesn't care?

Suffering isn't simply an intellectual problem. It's a very personal, emotional issue. God may be there, but we want to know if he cares.

All those friends I've talked about on this page would say, despite all they've been through: *Yes, God cares*. They say that because they are followers of Jesus. Here's why.

Jesus *shares* in our suffering

Jesus has experienced real suffering. In fact, Jesus has experienced agony. When he lived on earth, he knew what it was like to mourn, to be let down, and to be betrayed. He knew what it was like to be mistreated in his own home town. In his last days, he knew what it was like to be condemned to death, even though he was innocent. He knew what it was like to be tortured. He knew what it was like to be whipped and mocked, and then have nails about as tall as a large coffee mug driven through his hands, and then be suffocated for three hours.

The Bible even suggests that Jesus still knows what suffering feels like. Which is strange, since the Bible says Jesus now lives in heaven. When, months after he'd returned to heaven, Jesus spoke to someone who'd been persecuting Christians, he said:

"Why do you persecute *me*?" (Acts 9 v 4)

This suggests that when someone harms a Christian, Jesus feels the pain (just as when someone hurts someone you love, you feel the pain too). This makes Jesus unique among all the "gods" of all the various religions. Jesus is the only one who has suffered himself and knows what it's like.

As an old poem puts it: "Not a God has wounds, but thou alone". Jesus may not share with us all the answers we want about suffering. But there's one thing we do know: he knows how we feel. He knows because he's stood where we stand and cried as we cry. Whatever may be happening to us, Jesus knows how we feel and if we trust him, we're not alone.

This also means that grief and sadness are natural and normal parts of life following Jesus, because Jesus himself felt this way. The Bible never says it's wrong to grieve, to be frustrated or to be torn up inside. In fact sometimes it seems to say it's wrong *not* to feel like that. The Bible contains a collection of poems, called psalms, which give us examples of how to relate to God. And they often include anger, confusion and pain. In one of them,

Psalm 88, the writer seems literally to feel nothing good. He says to God:

> "I am overwhelmed with troubles
>> and my life draws near to death.
> I am counted among those who go down to the pit;
>> I am like one without strength …
>> darkness is my closest friend."   (Psalm 88 v 3-4, 18b)

The Bible is about real life. So it doesn't try to pretend that our existence is all sweetness and skipping. It says that there will be times when we might be sad; when we should be sad. There will be times when there are no easy answers. But it keeps on telling us that God knows how we feel, because he's felt it too.

That means that (even if you never have before) you can talk to God about what's going on: about your disappointments and worries, your hurts and your concerns. You can talk to him as someone who knows exactly what you're going through, because he's been through it all himself.

Jesus *helps* us in our suffering

Amazingly, the Bible even says Jesus helps his followers in their sufferings, by using them for their good. How strange does that sound? Suffering is used for good! Here are some words from the Bible:

> "We know that suffering produces perseverance;
> perseverance, character; and character, hope."
>
>> (Romans 5 v 3-4)

Suffering is a chance for a Christian to learn to persevere; to keep going when the going is tough. And perseverance impacts someone's character; it changes them. It leads someone to have a greater hope in who Jesus is and where they are headed. Suffering reminds a Christian that this world is broken, so they shouldn't love it too much; and it reminds them that they will one day be with

Jesus in a perfect world, so they should keep going with hope. It makes us realise that, however tough life may be, we'd rather face it with Jesus than without.

In the Bible, the word "hope" doesn't mean wanting something unlikely to happen, like: "I hope my local school team wins the Superbowl" or "I hope my gran wins *XFactor*". Instead it means certain confidence—knowing something good is definitely going to happen.

I do realise how irritating all that might sound if you're actually suffering. You might be thinking: "What planet is this guy on? He understands nothing of what I'm feeling! His mum isn't ill! He isn't being bullied! He hasn't failed his exams! How can he talk about growing through suffering?"

But remember those friends I talked about at the start of the chapter—they've really, really suffered. And they have let their suffering produce perseverance, character and hope. The question is not how much we suffer, but whether we let suffering bring us to God, and then let it increase our joyful confidence in the world to come; or whether we let it drive us away from God, and away from any real hope for the future.

One person I deeply admire is Drusilla Barron. You probably haven't heard of her, but she suffered the murder of most of her family, including her parents, when she was less than four. She then ended up in a foster home where she was repeatedly raped and abused by her foster father and most of the rest of the family. The pain she has experienced is unimaginable to me. But she has found healing in Jesus Christ. She calls these terrible events "weeds", and writes:

> "Jesus wants our weeds to transform [us], to recall us to whom he created us to be, because they are what we have to give and giving them to Him shows how much we love him."

A friend I know recently learnt that his new-born son is suffering from a serious disease that will probably cause a number of physical disabilities. Before the test results came back, my friend wrote a list of ten advantages of his son having this condition. They included:

- Easier to fix our eyes on Jesus and the hope that he brings
- Allows us to relate better to those who suffer
- Helps us to show that what really matters is knowing Christ
- Helps us to show the value of individuals with disability

To be honest, I don't know how I'd feel in these situations. But I know it's possible to see them as part of the way in which Jesus helps us—because I can see how these people have responded. Because they know Jesus, they have been able to face horrendous situations and yet find hope and even joy in knowing him.

Jesus *serves* us in suffering

Remember what I said in the first section about how Jesus knows what it's like to suffer? That's actually only half of the story. Jesus not only suffers with us—he suffered for us.

Jesus didn't simply come to earth so he would know what suffering feels like. That would just be patronising, a bit like a celebrity spending 24 hours living as a homeless person for a publicity stunt. No, Jesus came to suffer so that he could serve us. In fact, his suffering can save us.

Remember the amazing, perfect world we thought about in the previous chapter? There's a problem with it. Well, actually, there's a problem with us. None of us can ever get there by ourselves. It's a perfect world, and nothing imperfect can enter it. And so, since we all disobey God, we don't deserve to enjoy that world—we deserve only to be shut out of it. The punishment for choosing to live without God as our ruler in this world is that we don't get to live in it at all.

But amazingly, the Bible says that Jesus was punished instead of us. That's what was happening when Jesus suffered. When he died, he was suffering the punishment that we deserve, so we could have an amazing reward, which we could never deserve. The Bible puts it like this:

> "But he was pierced for our transgressions,
>   he was crushed for our iniquities;
> the punishment that brought us peace was on him,
>   and by his wounds we are healed.
> We all, like sheep, have gone astray,
>   each of us has turned to our own way;
> and the LORD has laid on him
>   the iniquity of us all."   (Isaiah 53 v 5-6)

This is one of the most surprising and wonderful truths in the Bible. Jesus died—he was crushed—in our place. And Jesus is God himself. God laid the punishment we deserve on... God. And that means that we can be at peace with him again. It means that our imperfections, our sins, can be taken away, and Jesus can give us his perfection, so that we can live in the perfect world we long for.

It means that you can enjoy a world without any pain, disappointment, fear or anxiety... for ever.

So does God care? He cares enough to leave heaven, live on earth, and die on a cross—for you. The Bible puts it like this:

> "God demonstrates his own love for us in this: while we
>   were still sinners, Christ died for us."   (Romans 5 v 8)

Whatever the songs we download off iTunes may tell us, love is not really all about feelings or all about sex. The reality is that love is about sacrifice. That sounds weird. But think about a good marriage. Think about the best marriage. It would be full of sacrifices—where both people didn't do what was easiest or nicest for them, so that they could do what was best or most joyful for the other. You'd see the husband staying up late to tidy up. You'd see the wife letting the husband watch what he wanted to on TV, and enjoying it with him. You'd see both of them putting the other first.

True love is sacrifice. Jesus has sacrificed himself and suffered agony for us. This is ultimate love.

So there are questions about suffering the Bible doesn't answer. But here's one the Bible answers over and over again, because it's the most important one of all:

Does God care?

The answer to that could not be clearer. He cares so much that he came and lived and died so that you can live in a world with no suffering, at all, ever.

That's all that the people I've mentioned in this chapter had to hang on to when suffering struck their lives. But that's all they needed. Maybe that's what you need to hang on to right now. Anyone can come to Jesus and be someone he died for, so that they can live with him for ever. Anyone can look at Jesus dying on the cross and say: "God cares".

6. Hasn't science disproved God?

I moved to a new house recently, and became the proud owner of lots of cheap, build-it-yourself furniture. I sat there faced with big pieces of wood, medium pieces of wood and little pieces of wood. I had plastic bolts, wooden bolts and metal bolts, drawer handles and bed-posts.

And I had no idea how they all fitted together.

This is when the instructions come in useful. Or sometimes come in useless. Because at this point, you can either choose to ignore the instruction manual, or read it. I chose to read it. But then you can choose to read the manual properly, or read it badly. If you read it well, it tells you what to do, in what order, with what pieces of equipment. If you read it badly, you find you've nailed your wardrobe door handle to the top of your bookshelf.

How you read an instruction booklet decides whether it helps or hinders you in understanding your furniture.

And science is a bit like that. Science is a way to find out about the world, using observation and experiments to gather information. It can either help us or hinder us in understanding our world, depending on how we interpret it. Here's one famous scientist, Richard Dawkins:

> "The universe we observe has precisely the correct
> properties you would expect if there is, at bottom, no
> design, no purpose, no evil and no good, nothing but
> blind, pitiless indifference."

In other words, Dawkins looks at science and says that it means there's no God. Maybe you agree with him.

But other people read science differently. Here's John Houghton, former Professor of Atmospheric Physics at Oxford University and former Chief Executive of the UK Meterological Office:

> "The size, the complexity, the beauty and the order we
> find in the universe are expressions of the greatness, the
> beauty and the orderliness of the creator."

Houghton looks at science and it leads him to believe in God. We've got two clever scientists—Dawkins and Houghton—looking at science and reading it completely differently. These days, even though millions still agree with Houghton, a growing number of people think Dawkins is reading science properly—that the more science we know, the more we realise there's no God.

It won't surprise you to know that I'm on Houghton's side of this debate. Why? Why do I think science shows us that God is there? That's what the rest of this chapter is about.

A wonderful world suggests a marvellous Maker

Science makes us go "Wow" at the world. Think of the complex maze of vessels carrying blood around your body so you're alive to read this book—wow! Think about the vast combination of tiny structures that make up the eyes which allow you to read this book—wow! Think about how birds and animals are wonderfully adapted to their environment; for instance, the *Epiphyllum* cactus flower has an eight-inch long tube-shaped flower, with the nectar at the bottom. The hawkmoth, which pollinates it, has a tongue eight inches long to reach the nectar. Wow!

Have you ever seen a sunset on a clear day, the whole sky lit up in beautiful hues of red and orange? Ever been walking in serious mountains and seen them tower above the landscape, like ancient, rocky kings and queens? Ever been far from any lights and looked up at the night sky and seen more stars than you could number, great and small, bright and dim, combining to make a perfect display of glimmering light?

These are things that make us say "Wow" about the world. And scientists are people who get to spend their days investigating them. A scientist holds a magnifying glass to our beautiful world and sees in more and more detail how "wow" it is.

How could such an amazing world get here? I think there are basically two answers you can give: random chance or deliberate creation. It's the same with everything: either something came about by accident or it was made deliberately. So, if there's really no kind of God at all, then the universe just happens to be here. It's just luck, a result of random chance. The thing is, though, that it's astoundingly unlikely that a universe anything like ours should come about by chance. One scientist has said it involves a one-in-a-million chance happening fifteen times in a row. Imagine covering the surface of the earth in 5p coins and painting one of them black. Now imagine flying up into space and firing a pin down at the earth. It is far, far more likely that the pin will land on the black coin than those 15 one-in-a-million chances come off.

This means that a universe more brilliant and beautiful than you could ever imagine has come into being, when any kind of universe like ours, let alone a brilliant and beautiful one, was crazily unlikely. To my mind, that suggests there was a deliberate Creator. Remember that flower with the eight-inch-long tube and moth with the eight-inch-long tongue? Maybe it looks like a match made in heaven because it *is* a match made in heaven! A wonderful world suggests a marvellous Maker. As the Bible puts it:

> "The heavens declare the glory of God; the skies
> proclaim the work of his hands." (Psalm 19 v 1)

This makes science even more exciting. Science is the way that we can find out more about how amazing God is, because he made everything and invented what we call science. Take the Oscar-winning film *Avatar*, directed by James Cameron. The special effects are mind-blowing. They make me think: "What a great movie-maker James Cameron is!" If you explained to me how the special effects worked, I wouldn't stop admiring James Cameron or think this was a film without a director. The more I knew how he'd made the film, the more I'd think he's a genius, and the more I'd love to meet him.

A brilliant film suggests there's a brilliant director. A wonderful world suggests a marvellous Maker.

But the world isn't always beautiful

Perhaps you're thinking: "Hang on, is the world really all that beautiful? What about all the war, disease, divorce and bereavement? What about my pain and misery? A lot in my world isn't beautiful!" That's a huge question, and we look at it in chapters four and five. But you're right—this world is beautiful, but it's also broken. Whatever we believe about it, we have to be able to explain both the good and the horrible. And the Bible explains that this world was created by God to be very good—beautiful—but it was wrecked by people not treating God's world, or God himself, as they should have; it got broken.

Imagine a piece of brilliant classical music. It's beautiful. But then a car alarm starts going off every minute, as the orchestra play. It ruins it. But it doesn't mean that the piece of music isn't lovely or didn't have a composer—it's just that the other sound is wrecking it. The Bible explains why we find this world fantastic, and why we discover that it's flawed.

Science tells us how, not who

Some people think that science can, or one day will, tell us everything. But in reality, there are things that science can't explain. Science is very good at telling us how things happen. It's not good at telling us who made them happen, and why.

Imagine you visit me and see the kettle boiling. You ask: "What's going on with the kettle?" I could give you the scientific answer— the "how" answer. The water is boiling because the electricity is causing the kettle's heating element to get warm, which in turn is causing the water particles to vibrate more, causing the water to reach 100^oC and start turning into gas.

But I could also give you the "who" and "why" answer: the water is boiling, because I want some coffee! Science would never work that out; a scientist can examine my kettle with microscopes, X-rays, Geiger counters and every instrument they've got, but they will never tell you that I'd like a cup of coffee.

Both answers are true, and both are important. The scientific answer is interesting, but it's not the only answer; and sometimes, it's not even the most important answer. Science tells us how the world works. It tells us about the natural processes that occur every day, sometimes unseen but always amazing. But it doesn't tell us who started those processes, or why.

This means that when a scientist claims that God doesn't exist, they've stopped doing science. The scientist examining my kettle can't tell you who turned it on. As far as science can tell, the kettle might have had one human owner, or several human owners, or maybe there is no human owner and a stone just happened to fall on the on-switch. It might be boiling because it was switched on by mistake, because I want a cup of coffee, or because I need to do some washing up and there's no hot water in the tap.

Science, by itself, can't prove or disprove any one of these answers. In the same way, it can't prove whether our world was made and is ruled by Jesus, Allah, a Time Lord, or no one. As soon as it answers "no one", instead of "I don't know", it's stopped being science.

But if science can't answer the "who" and "why" questions, then who can?

The ruler of science

Check out this account of Jesus, going on a boat trip with his friends:

> "A furious squall came up, and the waves broke over the
> boat, so that it was nearly swamped. Jesus was in the
> stern, sleeping on a cushion. The disciples woke him and
> said to him, 'Teacher, don't you care if we drown?' He
> got up, rebuked the wind and said to the waves, 'Quiet!
> Be still!' Then the wind died down and it was completely
> calm."   (Mark 4 v 37-39)

Jesus stops a raging storm… just by talking to it (check out chapter three if you think this is too far-fetched to believe). Imagine telling the water in your bath to stop moving, and it obeying. Impossible. Yet Jesus can control a whole sea! He can give orders to science and science obeys.

Think back to the scientist, examining my kettle. No matter how many tests they run, they can only find out how it works, not who turned it on. Now imagine I walk up to them and tell them I switched it on. There's the answer to the "who" question! Well, as we read about Jesus commanding wind and waves to shut up, and them doing as they're told, that's the answer to the "who" question when it comes to the world. Who made the world? Jesus. How does the world work? Through what we call science. Why did Jesus make the world? For our joy and his.

The patter of platypus' feet

Have you ever seen a duck-billed platypus? They live in Australia and they're pretty weird-looking animals. They have beaks like ducks, feet like otters and tails like beavers. I once heard that when the first stuffed specimens came back to Europe, people thought they were fakes and decided the animals didn't really exist. They'd never seen anything like it, and it just seemed too far-fetched!

So, picture this scene. A posh, old Victorian scientist is having a debate with an explorer. The scientist has many university degrees in science. He is seriously clever. The explorer spends more time in jungles than in libraries. He is seriously well travelled.

"Duck-billed platypuses don't exist," the scientist says. "Everything we know suggests the stuffed animals are obviously fakes. Where's the real evidence?"

"Here," says the explorer. And he opens the flap of a case under his arm. Out pops an animal. It's got a duck's beak, an otter's feet and a beaver's tail. It's a duck-billed platypus. It waddles over to the scientist, chirping cheerfully. It flaps its wet feet against his finely-woven trouser-legs.

The scientist quickly changes his mind.

This is what happens when Jesus enters our world. Jesus is God walking into a world that doesn't believe in him, like the platypus walking up to the scientist. Jesus is the evidence that there is a God who made everything. Jesus shows us how to "read" science, the manual for how the world works—he wrote it!

And that means the big thing I want to say, the main reason I think that science should lead us to praise God, is this: "Look at Jesus". Getting to know Jesus is getting to know as a friend the person who set up science. Science is amazing; and the guy who invented it is even more amazing than that.

7. What does Jesus really think about being gay?

When it comes to homosexuality, you could be forgiven for feeling confused about what Christians think. Some churches use offensive and aggressive language about gay people. Others openly celebrate same-sex weddings. Lots are somewhere in the middle. Thankfully, in the end it doesn't really matter what churches think. It's Jesus' opinion that's important. That's what this chapter is about.

But before we get going, can we ask you a favour?

In a world of tweets and Facebook status updates, it's easy to think we can deal with complex issues in a twenty-word sentence. But most things that are worth thinking about are more interesting, emotional and complicated than that. So please don't judge this chapter on an isolated sentence that catches your eye, but read the whole thing through, and think the whole thing through, before making up your mind.

Another little note before we start: sometimes we use the phrase "same-sex attracted". This is because a number of same-sex attracted people we know prefer this phrase to "gay", because "gay" implies being part of a lifestyle and a community, as well as just feelings. It's a bit clunky, but it's polite and respectful to use the longer term if some people prefer it.

But before we start to think about homosexuality, we want to think about identity.

You are...

Who are you? In one sense, that's a really easy question to answer. I'm Michael Dormandy. He's Carl Laferton. But in another sense, it's a surprisingly difficult question to answer. Michael Dormandy is just my name. It's not really who I am. So who actually am I? What sums up me? What sums up you?

For some people, *you are how you look*. Your value and self-worth as a person come from having the right wardrobe and a good body. So you avoid foods that you enjoy, and spend hours exercising or your weekends shopping, so that you look great.

For others, *you are what you do*. The job you do, the grades you get, the status you achieve in life; that's what matters. If that's you, you'll work all day, every day. Depending on what stage of life you're at, everything else will be sacrificed for the promotion, the job, the university place, the A*.

For others, *you are what you have*. Whether it's money, cars or gadgets, the most important thing about a person is the stuff they've got. Everything you are and everything you do will be about getting that little bit more.

For some people, *you are who you know*. You go to bed each night knowing your life is worth living because of the parties you get invited to, the connections you've made, the number of Facebook friends and Twitter followers you have. Every choice you make, from the clothes you wear to the things you do for fun, is aimed at getting into, or staying in, the in-crowd.

For others—actually for many of us—the answer is *you are who you sleep with*. What makes life worthwhile and satisfying and enjoyable is having lots of great sex. Whatever it takes to get that boy or girl into bed with you, you'll do it. And if you don't have anyone to sleep with, then somehow you've failed, and your life is boring black-and-white instead of exciting high-definition colour. If you are who you sleep with, and you have no one to sleep with, then there's not much point to you, is there?

There's one more answer to "Who are you?" When a Christian asks who they are, they let God answer the question. And God says:

> "In Christ Jesus you are all children of God through faith
> … and since you are his child, God has made you also an
> heir."   (Galatians 3 v 26; 4 v 7)

A Christian is a child of a perfect, powerful Father—God. They're part of a perfect, eternal family. They are beautiful in the eyes of the One who runs everything. One day, God will give them everything that is his—perfection, for ever. The amazing thing is that we don't have to do anything to get or keep this identity—it's given by God to anyone who asks him for it by trusting in Jesus.

This is the best news in the world. It means we don't have to worry about what we wear, what we do, what we have, who we know or who we sleep with. If we are trusting Jesus, we know exactly who we are. We're God's children.

People who understand this make amazing sacrifices in response; they give up other things if those things get in the way of enjoying being God's children. Not because they have to, but because they want to. Christians sometimes say "no" to things that look or feel good because they've found something better, or rather, they've found someone better.

This answer to "Who are you?" is one of the most important things in this book; and if you don't understand it, you'll never get what the Bible teaches about sex, relationships, or anything else, or why Christians make the choices they do.

So, what does Jesus say about sexuality? (By the way, this chapter will treat Jesus as God, and the Bible as being what Jesus says. We're guessing you may well have turned to this chapter first—in which case, it'd be great to keep an open mind about who Jesus is and what the Bible is and then, after reading this chapter, turn to chapters two and three, where those issues are looked at in more detail.)

What Jesus is saying

In the historical accounts of Jesus' life, we find him welcoming the marginalised, abused and bullied people of society. In his day, these people were the tax collectors and the prostitutes. He kept getting attacked by the upright, religious types for being "a friend of tax collectors and sinners" (Luke 7 v 34). Today, in many places, people who experience same-sex attraction are among the marginalised, abused and bullied people. So one thing's for sure—Jesus would have wanted to know them, welcome them and be friends with them. If you experience same-sex attraction or if you're in a same-sex relationship, be in no doubt: Jesus wants to know you and speak to you.

But one thing that's amazing about Jesus is that, while he welcomed people as they were, he didn't always say it was fine for them to stay as they were. He wanted people to see there was far more to life than what they wore, who they knew… and who they dated. And, because he's God, he also wanted people to realise that he knew how they could best enjoy and find satisfaction in life… and sometimes that would involve changing how they lived.

Jesus didn't talk that much about sex, perhaps because it was less of an issue for him and for people around him than it is in our culture today. But here's one thing he did say, when he was asked a question about marriage:

> "At the beginning the Creator 'made them male and female' and said, 'For this reason a man will leave his father and mother and be united to his wife, and the two will become one flesh.' So they are no longer two, but one flesh. Therefore what God has joined together, let no one separate." (Matthew 19 v 4-6)

When Jesus says "the two will become one flesh", that's a way of saying "two people will have sex". So in this one comment, Jesus is saying two massively controversial things about sex…

First, that sex is for marriage. He says that a man will be "united to his wife"—will get married—and then "the two will become one flesh". This is massively counter-cultural today—most people would say: "The two will become flesh, and then possibly, a while after that, if they want to, the man will be united to the woman in marriage". But it makes a lot more sense than you might think at first. Sex without unconditional commitment breeds insecurity and fear. "Am I good enough?" we ask. "Can I really trust that this person won't get out of bed afterwards and leave me lonely?" Marriage is the way we say: "I will still be here tomorrow, loving you, whatever happens. You don't need to worry." Within the safety and security of a marriage commitment, sex can flourish as an exciting and beautiful celebration of unconditional, lifelong love.

Second, Jesus says that sex is for a man and a woman. God made people "male and female", and getting united, or married, is about a man and a woman. The way God set up the world is for marriage to be between a guy and a girl. So while the Bible says close friendships between people of the same gender are great, it makes clear that (whether or not they involve sex) they're not marriages.

Of course, that's not how western culture today thinks about how the world should work. But it is what God says about how things should be, and it is why the Bible says that sexual relationships outside heterosexual marriage aren't right. The Bible occasionally calls these relationships "unnatural" and "shameful". These are powerful words; but in the Bible, what they mean is "against God's good plan". That helps us to understand why the Bible includes lines like this, describing the way the world is today:

> "Even their women exchanged natural sexual relations for
> unnatural ones. In the same way the men also abandoned
> natural relations with women and were inflamed with
> lust for one another. Men committed shameful acts with
> other men." (Romans 1 v 26-27)

That passage uses some strong language which is easily misunderstood today, so please read through the whole of this chapter before you judge what we're saying! This passage is making clear that sex between two men or two women is always contrary to God's plan and disobedient to his will. The Bible isn't simply ruling out abusive relationships, or one-night stands. There were long-term homosexual relationships in Jesus' time, just as there are today.

Neither is this passage only relevant for the time when it was written. Remember what Jesus said? He started by pointing back to the way God created things. In other words, he was outlining the relationships that God says are right for the world he's created, at all times and in all places.

God hasn't told us exactly why he's said this is how things should be, and it's certainly hard to hear. But as our Creator, God has the right to tell us how to live in his world; and because he's the all-knowing Creator, it's good that he tells us these things. God gives us the right to live how we choose, in all areas of our lives—what we say, what we do, how we use our bodies—but he himself has the right to be displeased and grieved with our choices.

So, we've seen what Jesus is saying about sexuality. But we also need to be very clear about what he isn't saying.

What Jesus is definitely *not* saying

Right after those verses about sexuality in Romans 1, the Bible continues to lay out ways in which people decide to reject God and live their own way. It mentions things like envy, deceit and gossip. The point is that, yes, homosexual sex is wrong, according to God. But it is no more wrong than envy, lying, gossiping, and so on.

This means that churches are wrong if they ever suggest that if you're gay, you're not welcome, or that you are twisted (unless they put themselves in the same category, because all of us are gossips, or boastful, or envious, and so on).

Also, everyone finds themselves wanting to do things that God has said are wrong (Jesus himself did). The Bible calls those desires temptations. It's not wrong to experience temptation, whether it's desiring someone of your own gender or anything else (and of course few people choose what gender they're attracted to). No one temptation is worse than any other; the crucial thing is whether we act on the temptation, or—like Jesus—resist it.

And it's well worth adding that the Bible never says that gay sex is bad for your health; that gay relationships can't be long-term and faithful; that gay people should be discriminated against; or that homosexuality is demonic. If you've heard any of those things from churches or Christians and been hurt by these cruel untruths, then all we can say is: we're sorry. We hope you'll feel able to listen to Jesus, even if you've been burned by listening to Christians. And we hope you'll find a church that takes the Bible seriously, and therefore takes both its standards and its command to love people seriously.

Because here's the thing: Jesus does say that some things are wrong. But he doesn't say those things to judge you, but because he loves you and wants what's best for you.

He knows you're so much more than who you sleep with. You're someone designed to know him, and be loved by him, and love him, and live under his good rule as the Creator.

Jesus definitely, clearly loves *you*

But hang on… how do you know Jesus wants what's best for you, even when he says hard things to you? How do you know God loves you, particularly if he's saying that some of your deepest hopes are wrong? Because:

> "God demonstrates his own love for us in this: while we
> were still sinners, Christ died for us."   (Romans 5 v 8)

Jesus Christ loves you enough to have died for you; he loves you enough to take all the punishment that all of us deserve for living in

God's world as though we knew best, with all the damage, seen and unseen, which that causes (chapter five has more about this really important idea). He loves you enough to offer you the identity of being a loved, secure child of God. There is no one else who is able and willing to go through all this to offer you all this.

The Bible says that this identity of being a child of God is the most important one you can have, and the only one that lasts for ever. In fact, in one striking part of the Bible, God says that the best marriage with the greatest sex is only a glimmer of the amazing relationship and love between Jesus and his people (Ephesians 5 v 21-33). So that means that you can have the most wonderful sex, and the most amazing marriage, and be missing out on something far better. And it also means that you may never have sex, and never be married, and yet you can enjoy something far better and longer lasting—the love of the God who died for you.

But you're saying that, if I'm gay, I should stay single and not have sex?!

In a word, yes. Some people who experience same-sex attraction find their feelings change and they start being attracted to the opposite sex; but the Bible never promises that, and the evidence suggests that therapy programmes that offer it aren't very effective.

We don't want to patronise anyone by minimising the hardness of this call. But there are two other things worth saying:

There's more to who you are than who you're with

Remember what we said at the start? Christians have a new answer to the question: "Who are you?" You aren't what you wear, what you know, what you do, what you have or who you're with. You are a beloved child of the Creator of the universe. That makes it easier if the answers to those other questions aren't very impressive—if we don't look great or know many popular people, if we haven't achieved much in this life or if we've never had sex or never been in a relationship.

One of the most surprising and amazing things I (Michael) noticed when, in my late teens, I first met committed Christians my age was that they made it very easy for me to say I didn't have a girlfriend. To my friends at school, if you weren't sleeping with at least a dozen women (or claiming you were), you were more or less a loser. With Christians, it was wonderfully different. I was loved because of who I was, not who I was dating. For me, that was life-changing, and I hope it will be for you, whatever your orientation.

There's more to serving Jesus than giving up sex

Following Jesus means giving up everything in order to gain everything.

Jesus once met a rich man and told him to give up all he had. When the rich man wasn't up for it, Jesus' disciples pointed out that they had given up everything to follow him. Jesus replied:

> "No one who has left home or brothers or sisters or
> mother or father or children or fields for me and the
> gospel will fail to receive a hundred times as much in this
> present age: homes, brothers, sisters, mothers, children
> and fields—along with persecutions—and in the age to
> come eternal life."   (Mark 10 v 29-30)

Every Christian gives things up to follow Jesus. For some Christians, that's harder than for others. Right now, some are giving up their lives because they know Jesus is more precious than life. They're in prison, being tortured, facing execution. Some are giving up their sex lives because they know Jesus is more special than sex—perhaps because they're straight and single, or same-sex attracted and single, or married but for some reason can't have sex with their husband or wife. For all of them that hardship may last a lifetime.

But see what Jesus says—that in this life, Jesus gives far more than any of his followers could ever give up, and then he gives life for ever. There are a number of Christians we know that are attracted to their own gender and have refused to act on that attraction and have found peace and joy. You can find some of their stories, and get in contact with them, at livingout.org. Here's what one of them has said: "Jesus offers what no same-sex partnership ever will. The greatest gift Jesus gives us … is Jesus."

And of course, just because you're not in a romantic relationship, it doesn't mean you can't enjoy deep, rewarding friendships. For lots of us, the physical aspect isn't the most important thing about a marriage or romantic relationship, and the Bible celebrates close, trusting friendships between people of the same gender. A friend of ours who experiences same-sex attraction, but has chosen to obey Jesus in this area, puts it like this in a book called *Is God Anti-Gay?*: "As a single man, I am grateful that I have been able to drop everything to spend time with friends in great need. It would not have been so easy if I were married. I'm thankful too for the wide range of friendships I've been able to cultivate."

So if you're finding the Christian life hard, if you're giving things up, then that's part of what it means to follow Jesus. And you'll find him giving you far more in return. And if you're a Christian who isn't finding life hard because you give things up, could it be that something is wrong? Perhaps God is calling you to make more sacrifices with your money, your time, your social standing… or your love life?

Could it be?

This has been a very hard chapter to write; and we're aware that it may well have been a much harder chapter for you to read, especially if you're in a same-sex relationship, or want to be; or you're struggling with same-sex attraction, and struggling alone and in fear; or you have friends or family who are gay. We know that, as two married guys, it's easier for us to believe this teaching on sex and relationships than it is for many others. So why not listen to the stories of some people who are same-sex-attracted but aren't acting on it because they are following Jesus? You could start at the website livingout.org, or by reading the book we mentioned on the previous page, written by a guy who knows exactly how it feels to experience same-sex attraction: *Is God Anti-Gay?* by Sam Allberry.

But for now, we want to say thank you so much for reading this far. Perhaps everything in you, and every circumstance of your life, as well as the society we live in, is telling you to turn your back on this Jesus who says that sex outside heterosexual marriage is wrong—to re-invent him or reject him completely.

That's understandable. But just as we end this chapter, let us ask you…

Could it be that Jesus is the God who can give you more joy and security than any relationship or any sex ever can, and give it to you for ever?

Could it be that Jesus loves you so much that he is willing to risk your rejection by telling you what is best for you rather than what you want to hear?

Could it be that Jesus loves you so much that he died for you, and wants to love you, perfectly, for ever?

Could it be that it is worth giving up anything—even a relationship, even sex—to be someone who is a child of God?

The Bible's answer to those questions is "yes". And if you think there's even a small chance that the Bible might be right, then we'd encourage you to keep thinking about Jesus and what he offers.

8. Surely you don't think there's only one true religion?

If you ever wanted to lose friends and become unpopular, how would you do it? There are a few possible tactics. Not showering for a week. Insulting people's clothes. Eating only garlic. These would empty your life of friends fast. But I've discovered something almost guaranteed to make you greatly unpopular within minutes. Just say this:

> "I think my religion is right, and that all the others are wrong."

I know this because I've done it. I remember one time at school, a friend asked me if, as a Christian, I believed it was a good thing to encourage followers of other religions to become Christians. I answered: "Yes". He looked at me with a mixture of disbelief and dislike. "That's out of order," he said.

And he's right, isn't he? Christians say that their religion is the only true one. And that seems arrogant and big-headed. How can anyone say: "I'm right, and you're all wrong. I'm fine, and all of you are not"?

It *is* out of order.

Jesus himself consistently criticised anyone who said they were better than anyone else. He once told a story about a guy who thought that he had all the answers, and was friends with God—but in fact the opposite was true. And he finished that story with these words:

> "All those who exalt themselves will be humbled."
>
> (Luke 18 v 14)

In other words, if you think too highly of yourself, if you think you're better than others, prepare to be proved wrong.

And yet Jesus' followers dare to say that Christianity is right, and other religions aren't. How can they say that? Why would they say that? Basically, it's because there is something unique about who Jesus is; and something unique about what Jesus can do.

Only Jesus is...

Jesus is the only religious leader I know about who actually said he was God. Here are some words he said in a conversation with some Jewish people:

> "'Very truly I tell you,' Jesus answered, 'before Abraham was born, I am!' At this, they picked up stones to stone him."
>
> (John 8 v 58-59)

This is strange. Abraham lived over 1,000 years before Jesus, and Jesus' words sound muddled up. Jesus says a sentence that seems grammatically nonsense and historically crazy, and then suddenly the people listening want to kill him! It seems a bit of an overreaction to Jesus getting his words the wrong way round!

But in fact, Jesus knew exactly what he was saying—he was making a massive claim about himself. Centuries before, a guy called Moses had asked God: "What should I tell people your name is?" God didn't answer: "God". He said: "I am who I am" (or "I am" for short). So here, Jesus is using God's name for himself, and is saying he's been alive for centuries. The people he's talking to find it so offensive that they want to kill him.

All the founders and leaders of the major world religions claim to know something about God; but only Jesus actually claimed to be God. Muhammad claimed to be a prophet and the Buddha claimed to be a wise teacher, but both would loudly and clearly say they weren't God. Jesus said he was; and he proved it by his miracles, his perfect life and, most of all, by his rising from the dead (flick back to chapter three for more details about this).

And if Jesus is God, then that makes what he says about God very different from what anyone else says.

Imagine you want to get to know me. You could make a few guesses. Maybe I have blond hair. Maybe I like peanut butter. This is a bit like people who try to think about God for themselves. It's just a guess… you can never know for sure… and it'd be very arrogant to say that your guess is better than anyone else's.

Maybe you would decide to do more than guess about me, though. Maybe you'd find some people who said they knew me. But you've still got some problems. What if they don't really know me? What if they do, but they make a mistake about what I'm like? It's still all just guesswork; and you'd still be arrogant to say you knew better than someone else what I'm like.

Now imagine that you hear a ring on your doorbell. When you answer it, you see a tall, thin man with glasses and frizzy dark hair. He says: "I'm Michael Dormandy, one of the authors of the book you've been reading". It's me! And I prove it by it showing you my passport.

Until now, you've been dealing with guesses. Now you can know. You've met Michael, rather than people's ideas about Michael. You've met the truth; and actually, it would now be quite arrogant to look at me and say: "No, you're not Michael, because I think Michael has short, ginger hair"; "No, you're not Michael, because my friend says Michael doesn't wear glasses."

Jesus is God; he said it and proved it. So when it comes to getting to know God, Jesus is the only way to know for sure what he's like.

What Jesus says about God is right—even if other people think differently.

And so Christianity is all about certainty, not guesswork, because it's all about Jesus—God, come to meet us.

Only Jesus can...

Jesus isn't just the only religious leader who can truly show us God; he is also the only religious leader who can save us from our deepest problem. Look at this account of a dinner he went to:

> "While Jesus was having dinner at Levi's house, many tax collectors and sinners were eating with him and his disciples, for there were many who followed him. When the teachers of the law who were Pharisees saw him eating with the sinners and tax collectors, they asked his disciples: 'Why does he eat with tax collectors and sinners?'" (Mark 2 v 15-16)

Jesus is accused of spending too much time with society's nobodies (this Levi was a tax collector—a traitor and thief—not the guy who invented the jeans). The people Jesus hung out with were the thieves, the prostitutes, the bad guys. The religious leaders— the Pharisees—didn't like this at all. Surely Jesus should choose to spend his time with good, well-behaved people? Here's how Jesus answered them:

> "It is not the healthy who need a doctor, but those who are ill. I have not come to call the righteous, but sinners." (Mark 2 v 17)

Jesus came to be a doctor for sick people. By sick, he meant the fact that we're "sinners". Sin is our refusal to accept that God is God, and our failure to love each other. That's an illness that everyone has. (Let's be honest, neither I nor you live up to our own standards, let alone God's perfect ones.) And it's an illness which has a terminal outcome; if we don't get better, we face God's anger, and an eternity without him and without anything good.

The sick need a doctor—and Jesus is saying that when it comes to sin, he's the doctor, the one who can heal this disease. Jesus came to offer to take away the result of our sin—God's judgment—and to work in us to get rid of our sin.

Again, this puts Jesus in a different category.

Other religions don't claim to heal this sin-disease. Buddhism admits that all the Buddha did was suggest beliefs and disciplines that can show you how to reach the goal of complete contentment and peace. I'm sure many of these disciplines succeed in bringing a sense of contentment. But they can't get rid of the disease of sin. That would be like trying to cure cancer by taking vitamins each day. And a number of Islamic websites admit Muslims can't ever be sure they'll go to heaven. This is like a doctor admitting they don't know if they can cure the cancer.

All the religions of the world suggest health tips; and they sometimes include some excellent health tips. But most of them suggest ways to make yourself better, and just as you can't cure your own cancer, you can't cure your own sin.

Jesus is different. Doctor Jesus doesn't tell us what to do to be healthy; Jesus surgically removes the cancer. Only Jesus really deals with sin.

Jesus takes on church-ianity

There's one self-cure religion that looks really great, and is very popular in the western world. I know that, because I used to be part of it.

I call it "church-ianity".

It's very easy to go to church, sing hymns and enjoy the buildings… but still rely on your own guesses about God, rather than listening to Jesus. And it's very easy to go to church, do good things and try to obey God… but be relying on these things to cure your sin-disease.

But only Jesus can save, not church. Going to church doesn't cure you. Trying very hard to obey the Ten Commandments doesn't cure you. Only Doctor Jesus can do that.

Sometimes people are into church-ianity for many years before they meet Jesus, the cancer-curing master-surgeon. Look at these words from the Christian leader, Paul, who was just like that:

> "If someone else thinks they have reasons to put confidence in the flesh, I have more: circumcised on the eighth day, of the people of Israel, of the tribe of Benjamin, a Hebrew of Hebrews; in regard to the law, a Pharisee; as for zeal, persecuting the church; as for righteousness based on the law, faultless.

> "But whatever were gains to me I now consider loss for the sake of Christ. What is more, I consider everything a loss because of the surpassing worth of knowing Christ Jesus my Lord, for whose sake I have lost all things. I consider them garbage, that I may gain Christ."

(Philippians 3 v 4-8)

Paul topped the charts for ancient-times church-ianity. He was from the most pure religious family, top of his class in Religious Education and regular winner of the "most religious boy in school" prize (in those days, that was a top award). But when he met Jesus, he said all that was "garbage". In the language Paul originally used, the word also means "excrement". Paul is saying that compared to Jesus, church-ianity is like the stuff we flush down the toilet.

I have a similar story: I started off deep into church-ianity. I grew up in a traditional church. I sang the songs; I said my prayers. I thought I could be good enough to make God like me, but I kept failing. I thought I could cure myself; but I couldn't.

Then, when I was 16, someone told me that Jesus said I couldn't cure myself, but that I didn't need to; he'd do it for me, so that I could enjoy living with him, and look forward to perfection for ever.

I was so excited to meet Dr. Jesus. I traded in a religion for a rescue.

Religion or rescue?

We all have the cancer of sin. Of course, we can choose to deny we have it. We can pretend we're fine, and refuse to listen to the expert (Jesus). But that doesn't make the problem go away.

Or we can accept we've got a problem, and decide to heal ourselves. A devout Buddhist following their disciplines is a self-healer. So is little teenage me, saying the Lord's Prayer each night. So, actually, is anyone who thinks: "I'll be alright; I've never done anything too bad in my life—I'm sure I'm fine with God".

Or we can pick someone or something that we hope can cure us. This is what a Muslim is doing, who hopes Allah, in his mercy, will forgive them. The problem is, as we saw earlier, that Jesus said he was the only surgeon who could heal us, and he must be right because he's God.

But there is a fourth option: we can realise we've got a problem, realise we can't cure ourselves, and realise that only Jesus can cure us. He's God, so he gets to say what's right and wrong about God. And he's the doctor, so he can cure us of our sin and give us life for ever. We can come to Jesus and say: "Operate on me, please."

This is why, in many ways, Christianity isn't a religion; it's a relationship. It's calling Dr. Jesus.

Unpopular

It's not popular to say that Christianity is the only way to eternal life. And it would be arrogant to say that; unless Jesus is God. Remember Jesus' words from the start of this chapter?

"All those who exalt themselves will be humbled…"

Because Jesus is God, as he said and proved, then to ignore him and decide we know better is very big-headed. Because Jesus is God, to think we can save ourselves and don't need him to do it is also very big-headed.

But because Jesus is God, he was telling the truth when he finished that sentence:

"… and those who humble themselves will be exalted."

It takes humility—the opposite of arrogance—to accept that when Jesus and you disagree, Jesus is right. It takes humility to accept that you have a sin-disease that you can't cure yourself, and that you need Jesus Christ to do it for you. It takes humility to do these things —but they lead to you being "exalted"; to being a precious friend of God, with a place in his family and a place in his perfect future. True humility is to reject religion and come to Christ.

9. Why should *I* bother with Jesus?

I have never been very good at sport. In fact, I have always been appallingly, laughably bad. But, though I'll never get the chance to find out, I've always thought that sporting success would bring popularity, pleasure and fun. If you were at the top of the world in sport, imagine how cool that would be!

Except that at least one person who did get the chance to find out has discovered that it doesn't work like that. Andre Agassi is one of the tennis greats—he won eight Grand Slam events and an Olympic gold medal, and earned over $31,000,000. The night he first became world Number One, a reporter rang to ask him how he was feeling. "Great," he replied. Of course you'd feel great! But, as Agassi later wrote:

> "It's a lie. This isn't at all what I feel. It's what I want to feel. It's what I expected to feel, what I tell myself to feel. But in fact I feel nothing … I did it—I'm the number one tennis player on earth, and yet I feel empty. If being number one feels empty, unsatisfying, what's the point?"

Agassi had it all—but there was still something missing. It's actually quite a common feeling—we work for and dream about getting something, or being someone, and then we achieve it and… we find ourselves thinking: "Is that it?" So we find something else, something new or bigger or better, and we try to achieve that, in the hope that one day we'll say: "This is IT!"

Agassi had been striving to be the best tennis player in the world. The guy we're going to meet in this chapter, as we look at a single episode from one of the Gospel accounts of Jesus' life, had been working for something very different.

Meet Zacchaeus

> "Jesus entered Jericho and was passing through. A man was there by the name of Zacchaeus; he was a chief tax collector and was wealthy. He wanted to see who Jesus was, but because he was short he could not see over the crowd. So he ran ahead and climbed a sycamore-fig tree to see him, since Jesus was coming that way."
>
> (Luke 19 verses 1-4)

Unlike modern books which tell you everything about the characters, from the colour of their clothes to what they had for breakfast, the writers of the Bible don't go into detail to describe people, so often the pieces of description you do get are significant. Here, we're told that Zacchaeus was rich. And we're told why he was rich: he was a chief tax collector.

In Jesus' time, tax collectors took a large cut of the taxes for themselves, so they became very rich by stealing. Not only that— they also represented the Roman Empire, which was occupying the area where Jesus lived. So tax collectors were hated as traitors, a bit like French people who worked with the occupying German army in World War II.

Zacchaeus is a man who's traded in his honesty and his reputation, so that he can get rich. Why?! Well, there are at least two reasons why people really want money. It offers satisfaction and security.

Money seems to give satisfaction because it can get us whatever we think we need. Money is the path to fun things to do, amazing food, great parties, popularity, great relationships... all we need to enjoy life.

Money also seems to give us security, because if we have money we'll be OK. Nothing too much can go wrong, because my savings will always cushion me. I can buy myself out of whatever crisis hits. If I can just get good enough grades, to get a good enough job, with a good enough salary, I'll be OK.

The problem is... *money just doesn't deliver.* You can have as much money as you like, but it can't actually buy you love, or happy memories, or a clean conscience. It doesn't ever really satisfy. Agassi's millions still left him feeling empty. And you can have as much money as you like, but it can't actually buy you good health, and it certainly can't buy you a way out of death. It doesn't really ever give security.

In fact, whatever we look to in life to give us satisfaction and security—money, being top of the tennis rankings, a career, a relationship, an exam grade, a good car, whatever—it will never quite deliver.

Sooner or later, like Agassi, we'll realise we gained what we thought would make us satisfied and secure, and yet... we just feel a bit empty. And that's a problem for you and me, because all of us are looking to something that we believe, deep down, will make us satisfied and secure.

As we've seen, Zacchaeus' something was money. He'd thought money could give him everything—but he'd realised that he needed something more. How do we know? Because when Jesus was passing through, Zacchaeus didn't stay at home, counting his coins. Instead, "he wanted to see who Jesus was". And he was so determined to see this Jesus that he gave up his dignity, climbed a tree, and waited for him to come by.

Meeting satisfaction and security

When Jesus reaches Zacchaeus, he looks up at him, this rich guy perched in a tree, and says:

> "Zacchaeus, come down immediately. I must stay at your house today." (v 5)

Jesus wants to be friends with him! That's why he calls him by his name. That's why he calls him to come down. That's why he invites himself to stay in his house. Jesus is inviting Zacchaeus to make him a serious part of his life.

And Zacchaeus "came down at once and welcomed him gladly" (v 6).

Why is Zacchaeus so glad? Because this is a great day for him! It's the day his search for satisfaction and security are over. He hasn't found them by having bags of gold in his house and loving them in his heart. He's found them by welcoming Jesus into his house and his heart.

Only Jesus really gives satisfaction—the joy of knowing that God loves you and is helping you and is making sure your life counts, no matter what happens. Only Jesus really gives security—the joy of knowing that ahead of you lies not death and the end, but a beautiful life which will "never perish, spoil or fade" (1 Peter 1 v 4).

Zacchaeus is just beginning to find out why it's worth bothering with Jesus. Nothing and no one else will ever quite give you what you are looking for in life; and nothing and no one else can come close to giving it to you for ever. But Jesus can, and does.

Why should Jesus bother with *you*?!

But there's a huge problem here. On the one hand, you've got Zacchaeus, the traitor and thief, a man who has bent and broken most of the rules. On the other hand, you've got Jesus, who claims to be God living on earth. The question isn't why would Zacchaeus bother with Jesus, but why would Jesus bother with him? How can

God look at all the lying and cheating Zacchaeus has done and say: *It doesn't matter—I want to stay in your house as your friend?*

That's the question the people have as Zacchaeus climbs down the tree:

> "All the people saw this and began to mutter: 'He [Jesus] has gone to be the guest of a sinner.'" (v 7)

Why didn't Jesus just leave this nasty little man up his tree? How could he ask him to come down? Well, the clue is in the very first sentence of the episode: "Jesus entered Jericho and was passing through". He was passing through… to Jerusalem. And in Jerusalem, Jesus would climb his own tree—not a leafy, living tree, but a stark cross of death. Jesus would die on that cross to pay the penalty that men like Zacchaeus deserved for their wrongdoing, for what the Bible calls sin: "He himself bore our sins in his body on the tree" (1 Peter 2 v 24).

The only reason Zacchaeus could come down from his tree was because Jesus climbed his own tree. The only reason Zacchaeus could be friends with Jesus, and enjoy the satisfaction and security of that friendship, was because Jesus bore the weight of Zacchaeus' sins. Jesus died to pay the penalty for all Zacchaeus' cheating and stealing, all his looking to money for satisfaction and security.

Here's another reason you and I need to bother with Jesus. We have all done wrong. None of us are perfect. All of us have ignored and disobeyed God one way or another as we chase what we think we need in life. And someone has to pay the penalty for that. Money can't. Sporting success can't. Popularity can't. Jesus can. He was bothered enough about you to climb his cross for you.

The difference Jesus makes

Once you've met Jesus, it makes every difference to everything! Remember Zacchaeus, the money-grabbing, traitorous tax collector? Here's what he does now he knows Jesus:

> "Look, Lord! Here and now I give half of my possessions to the poor, and if I have cheated anybody out of anything, I will pay back four times the amount." (v 8)

Because he knows Jesus, and knows satisfaction and security come from Jesus, he doesn't need to be penny-pinching anymore. Instead, he can be generous. It's a complete change in his attitude to money. Money isn't in charge of his life anymore; Jesus is—that's why he calls him "Lord".

This is what happens when we meet Jesus. Instead of trying to get everything, we can happily give anything. We're free to be generous. We're free to be thoughtful. We're free to enjoy life.

Why bother with Jesus? Because, as Zacchaeus found, satisfaction and security are promised by lots of things, but delivered by none except Jesus. And because only Jesus loves you enough to climb a tree and take the penalty for your sins. And because only if you know Jesus are you free to live a joyful life of generosity, thoughtfulness and love, knowing you'll enjoy that life for ever.

Finding yourself in the story

Where are you in this story of Zacchaeus meeting Jesus?

Maybe you've climbed the tree like Zacchaeus. Like him, you wanted to know a little bit about Jesus, so you picked up this book. But you've still got questions and this book hasn't answered them. In a sense that's not surprising—there are enough books to fill a library on each of the topics we've spent only a chapter on! Do keep thinking, do keep looking at Jesus—grab a Christian friend and ask them your questions. And why not look at Jesus properly by reading one of the accounts of his life in the Bible, one of the four "Gospels".

But of course, Zacchaeus didn't stay up his tree. Jesus called him down; and he came down and welcomed him. *Maybe* you've been looking at Jesus, but now the time has come to welcome him into your life as your Lord. You don't know all the answers to all your questions, but you want to know Jesus. You start doing that by trusting him and trying to do what he says. Many people begin by praying a prayer like this one:

> Dear Jesus,
> Thank you for the wonderful world you've made.
> I'm sorry that I have looked for satisfaction and security in places where I can't find them. I'm sorry that this has hurt me, you and other people. I'm sorry that I've been disobeying you.
> Thank you that you bore my sins in your body on the cross, and that you want to be in charge of my life.
> I am welcoming you in.
> Please help me to trust you and follow you as my Lord.
> Amen.

If you say that prayer and mean it, then you can know that Jesus has come into your life, taking your sins and bringing you eternal life. A great next step to take would be to join a church, where you can learn more about Jesus, get to know others who are following him, and serve him.

Or *maybe* you came down the tree to welcome Jesus as your Lord a while ago. I hope this book has helped you think through some of the questions you have, and some of the questions your friends might have.

Wherever you're at, I hope this book's given you some helpful answers. But more than that, I hope it's introduced you to Jesus.

The best thing in the world is not knowing all the answers. It's knowing Jesus.

Other great books about Jesus and what it means to follow him...

LOST

When the Dream turns to a Nightmare

A son turns his back on home and family to follow his dreams of a new life on his own. Another son stays dutifully at home.

But **when the dream turns to a nightmare**, what will this first son do? And which of the two sons is really the more lost?

In this deceptively simple story, Jesus gets to the heart of what it means to be lost to God, and found by him again. And it's a story that's **full of surprises**.

You'll be surprised by the father, surprised by the sons, and surprised by what this story tells us about our own hearts.

And there there's the biggest surprise of all... **Jaw-dropping in fact...**

Jonty Allcock is the pastor of Bush Hill Park Community Church in North London. He rides a six-foot unicycle and plays the saxophone. He is married to Linda and they have three (noisy) boys.

HERO

When an ordinary person meets an extraordinary God

Turn upside down everything you knew about fame and significance. Discover what happens when God takes hold of loser-boy Gideon and moulds and shapes him into the unlikeliest of heroes; and how God continues to use weak people to work for him in his world.

FEARLESS

Standing firm when the going gets tough

Turn upside down everything you knew about bravery, as you find out how Daniel and his mates were able to stand firm under pressure. Discover what you need to know about God and his plans in order to live in a way that is courageous instead of cowardly.

Available from most Christian retailers or direct from:

UK: www.thegoodbook.co.uk
North America: www.thegoodbook.com
Australia: www.thegoodbook.com.au
New Zealand: www.thegoodbook.co.nz

And two things to help you get started with reading the Bible...

explore

Explore daily devotionals

These notes, written for people of every age and stage, take you to a particular part of the Bible, and through a mixture of questions and comments help you think it through, see what it means for your life, and pray about it. You can buy a paper copy, or download the app.

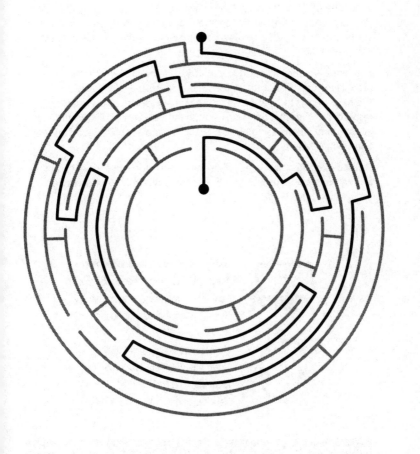

thegoodbook
COMPANY
Opening up the Bible

At The Good Book Company, we are dedicated to helping people think about the Christian faith and their own views, and to helping Christians and local churches grow. We believe that God's growth process always starts with hearing clearly what he has said to us through his timeless word—the Bible.

Ever since we opened our doors in 1991, we have been striving to produce resources that honour God in the way the Bible is used. We have grown to become an international provider of user-friendly resources to the Christian community, with believers of all backgrounds and denominations using our Bible studies, books, DVD-based courses and training events.

If you'd like to know more, call us for a discussion of your needs or visit one of our local websites for more information on the resources and services we provide.

UK & Europe: www.thegoodbook.co.uk
North America: www.thegoodbook.com
Australia: www.thegoodbook.com.au
New Zealand: www.thegoodbook.co.nz

UK & Europe: 0333 123 0880
North America: 866 244 2165
Australia: (02) 6100 4211
New Zealand: (+64) 3 343 1990